All photography by Katsuhiko Tokunaga©,
with the following exceptions:
Squadron Leader Andy Stewart:- pages 20-21, 22, 25,
28-29, 30-31, 40-41, 53, 56-57, 66-67, 84-85, 89, 119, 126-127.
Andy Fountain:- pages 112, 113, 114, 115, 117.
Written by Squadron Leader Andy Stewart.
Designed by Pavilion Communication Services Ltd.
Design Co-ordinator Sarah Rochford.

ISBN 0-86124-914-3

CONTENTS

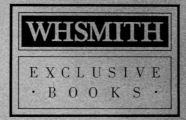

WHSMITH

EXCLUSIVE
· BOOKS ·

PP10 and 11 *Over the top in "9 Arrow", with Reds 6 and 7 (the Synchro Pair) flying immediately behind the Leader. Note Red 6's rudder in the Leader's smoke, and therefore jetwash, showing how "shallow" the correct position is when flying in line astern.*

PP12 and 13 *Look again, that's Synchro 2 crossing from left to right! The airbrake (under the tail) is extended to keep the speed under control against the high engine power setting, needed to ensure the intensity of the coloured smoke.*

Above *The Synchro Pair pull up and out of the formation to begin the second half of the display. With the main section of seven in "Leader's Benefit" and about to pull up into their own loop, Synchro will next form "The Heart" (see P62).*

Right *Having detached from the other seven aircraft, this is the moment just before Synchro "Split." Each will roll his aircraft through 90 degrees away from the other, and then pull over the top to form a lobe of the heart shape.*

RED ARROWS –
THE BACKGROUND

Since the days of the Hendon Air Displays in the 1920s and 30s, the RAF has had a reputation for excellence in flying formation aerobatics. Indeed in the 1950s almost every fighter squadron and training unit was represented by its own formation team. Only in 1965, however, was a squadron formed with the unique purpose of becoming *the* Royal Air Force Aerobatic Team. The Red Arrows Squadron was established under the command of the Royal Air Force Central Flying School (the oldest in the world) and for 16 years flew the Folland Gnat. These aircraft were painted red in recognition of the association with the CFS, which has a red pelican depicted on its official crest, and the name derived naturally both from the arrow-like shape of the Gnat aircraft and also from our famous forebears, the 111 Squadron Hawker Hunter display team, the Black Arrows.

Initially, all of the pilots on the Team were flying instructors chosen from within the CFS. Although it is no longer a necessary qualification for selection, each of today's pilots is, in fact, either a Qualified Weapons or Flying Instructor.

The Red Arrows first performance was at Biggin Hill in 1965, since which time we have flown in excess of 2500 shows in 45 different countries. This impressive number was achieved when the Team visited the Soviet Union for the first time in 1990. The display season extends from May until mid October each year and in those 5½ months we can usually expect to fly about 100 displays.

The aircraft used by the Red Arrows since 1980 is the versatile British Aerospace Hawk. In RAF service, the Hawk has two main peacetime roles. It is flown at the Advanced Flying Training School to train potential fast jet pilots, whilst at the two Tactical Weapons Units the Hawk is used to teach weaponeering and tactical skills before a pilot is posted to his front line aircraft.

Above Formation flying is a basic skill, learnt by every RAF pilot, to be used as a matter of routine. Its value as a crowd puller has, however, been recognised since the early days of aviation. Gloster Gladiators of No 19(F) Squadron.

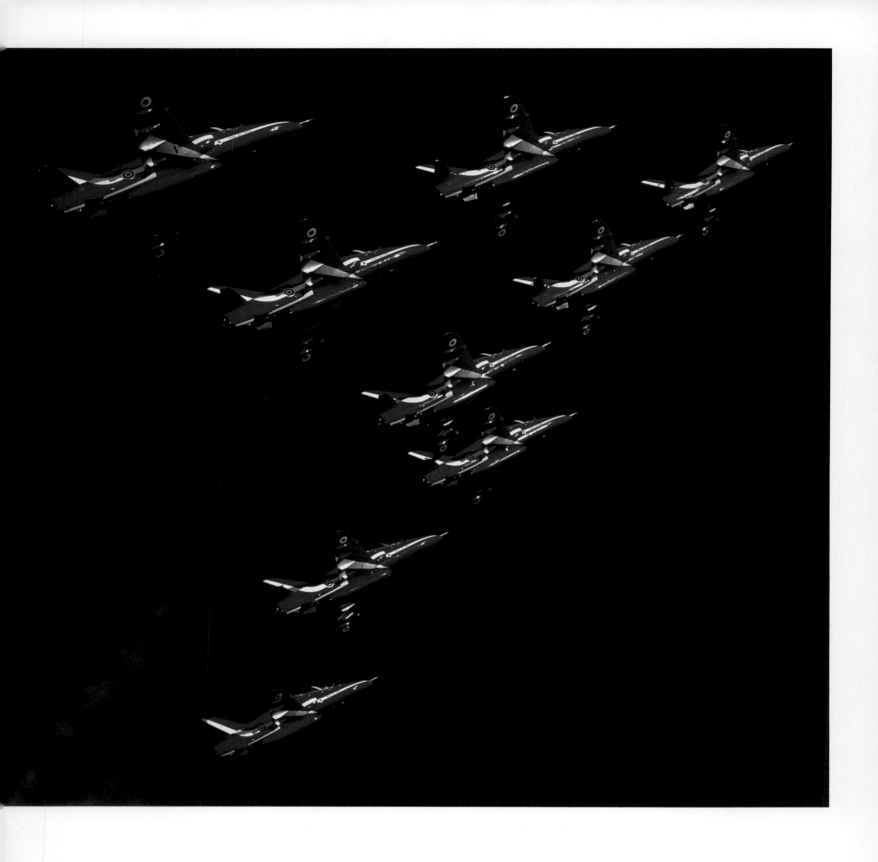

Above *"Eagle". Pulling up into a loop in the formation named after the lunar landing craft that first took man to the moon.*

Opposite *"Card." An especially difficult formation to get just right. Emulating the design on a playing card, this is the only shape that could be said to have changed the famous "Diamond Nine" into the "Nine of Diamonds."*

PP20 and 21 *"Cyprus Dawn." It is 0600 hours (0400 BST!) and the first training session of the day is about to get underway.*

Left The annual spring detachment to Cyprus affords the Team the opportunity to train in near ideal weather conditions, as can be appreciated in this dramatic picture postcard of the Cyprus coastline!

Below The "Rolling" and "Flat" displays come to a colourful climax with the "Vixen Break," an impressive manoeuvre that always gets camera shutters firing at air shows. At this instant the pilots are pulling 7G.

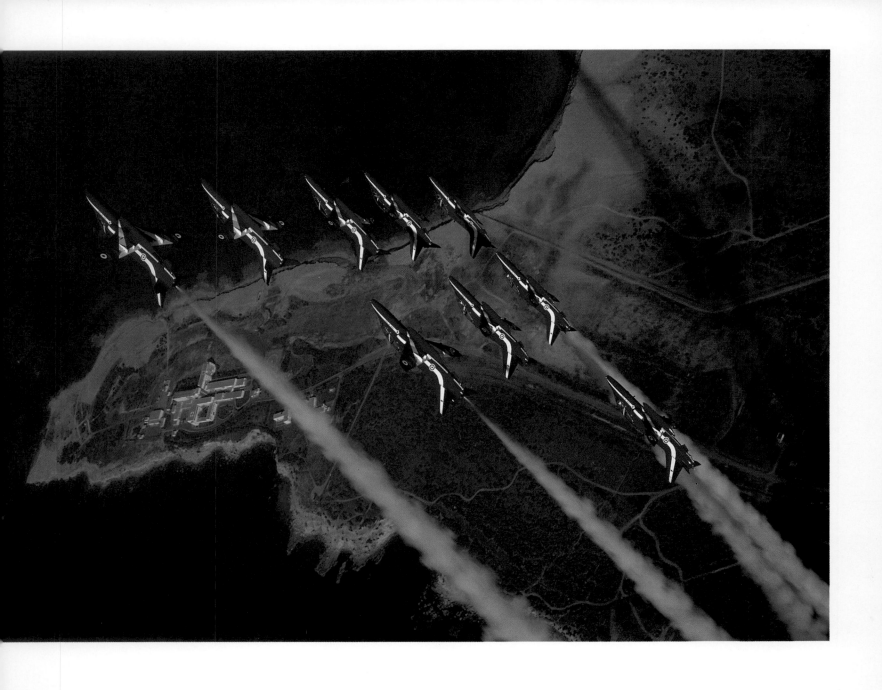

Above *The Princess Mary's Royal Air Force Hospital in Cyprus makes an unusual backdrop as the Team rolls in "Delta," which has been described as a triangle flying backwards! Nevertheless, no other Team rolls more than five aircraft in line abreast.*

Above *Still in Cyprus, the citrus groves pass close below Red 3, who concentrates on holding his position accurately with reference to the Leader's aircraft. Many "references" are used by each pilot during a display, such that each different formation shape appears symmetrical from the ground.*

THE SQUADRON

The Royal Air Force Aerobatic Team is an established RAF Squadron with the primary role during peace time of demonstrating the teamwork and excellence of performance demanded of all RAF personnel. However, in time of war the red aircraft would be camouflaged, armed with 30mm cannon and Sidewinder missiles and flown by the ten pilots to augment the UK Air Defence forces.

The nine display pilots and the flying Team Manager have varying backgrounds and are a cross-section of the RAF's fast-jet aircrew. Between them they have amassed some 24,000 flying hours and each has normally served in the RAF for at least 10 years. A tour on the Red Arrows lasts 3 years, after which the pilots return to the front line or instructional duties. For many, however, the end of their tour coincides with the end of their military service, enabling them to pursue a second career out of uniform. The changing of three pilots each winter provides the best compromise between the injection of "new blood" and the maintenance of a stable, experienced foundation on which to build next year's display.

Successful planning and organisation of each display is vital if ten aircraft, support equipment and travelling engineers are to arrive safely and fully prepared at a display venue. Planning for each show in the coming season starts as soon as the previous year is over.

Each display has its own organisational constraints and one show is therefore rarely the same as the next. Typically, accommodation and catering facilities will be required for up to 50 personnel and the Team's aircraft will require fuel and other local assistance arranged well in advance – both at home and overseas. A sense of humour and the ability to remain flexible are vital as amendments to this detailed planning can occur literally hours before take-off, while arrangements for forthcoming displays still need to be considered and finalised throughout the season, as part of an ongoing administrative system.

The task of coordinating these elements falls to the Manager and to the Team Adjutant, whose staff prepare the

Operation Orders and complex paperwork associated with each display. The team also has an Assistant Air Traffic Controller who works closely with the two navigation officers, Red Arrows pilots Nos 4 and 5, in the preparation of routes, maps and timings for each display.

Typically three weeks before a display the show organiser will have been provided with a detailed document showing timings, transit routes, personnel involved and equipment required. Ten aircraft are flown to the operating airfield, the spare aircraft piloted by the Manager.

The travelling Team Engineering Officer and nine specialist technicians, called the "Circus", fly in the rear seats of the Hawk aircraft to the forward operating bases (which are often not the display locations) so that essential servicing can begin before either the support aircraft or the road support party arrives. A Hercules aircraft or a road convoy transports spares, servicing equipment and the remaining 17 engineering personnel.

Before all displays the pilots are briefed by the Team Leader on prevailing weather, obstacles, the display sequence and any other vital information passed back by the Manager, who will by now have deployed to the actual display location by light aircraft, helicopter or by road. Once "on site", Mange (as he is known by the rest of the Team) becomes the Ground Safety Officer in 2 way radio contact with the pilots. He then gives the display commentary while the Team photographer videos the entire sequence so that it may be critically analysed and discussed by the pilots in the debrief after the display.

During the display season, travelling team members cannot expect to spend more than 2 days a week back home at RAF Scampton. Even this period is active with time spent replenishing stocks of spares and publicity material, servicing the aircraft and making the final arrangements for the next event. The frenzied activity and constant travelling does not stop until mid-October when most members of the Squadron take a welcome break before the winter training begins again.

PP28 and 29 "Double Take." One of those happy photographic accidents and an unplanned double exposure. The flypast was over Dover (note the White Cliffs!) and the self portrait was taken on landing.

PP30 and 31 Another "Twizzle" (see PP4-7) but this time rolling left as viewed from the tail end of the formation.

Opposite The classic "Diamond Nine," instantly recognisable as the trademark formation of the Red Arrows.

Above "Half Swan," flown slowly and with the undercarriage down, giving onlookers the opportunity to see the Hawk in its landing configuration.

PP34 and 35 Who says loops are round? The Synchro Pair having departed, the main section fans out in the "Cascade," with the early morning Cyprus sun as a spectacular backdrop.

Left An amazing view of the "Caterpillar Loop" with the aircraft having pulled up one after the other, from a line astern formation. This is the perspective you get if you lie on your back in the middle of the runway and look straight up!

Above The Synchro Pair must be the two most photographed aircraft at air shows!

PP38 and 39 The main section prepares for the "Goose." Flying relatively slowly (200MPH) with the undercarriage lowered, they leave a gap in the smoke through which the Synchro Pair will pass as they fly towards the rising sun.

PP40 and 41 The smoke is formed by introducing diesel fuel into the hot exhaust gases, where it vapourises. The addition of red or blue dye produces the distinctive coloured smoke. This picture was taken from the outside right of Apollo.

PP42 and 43 "Big Vixen," taken from Red 10 over the top, with the sea below.

PP44 and 45 Sunlight and sea make a spectacular backdrop for another air to air view, this time of the Diamond Nine in a left hand turn.

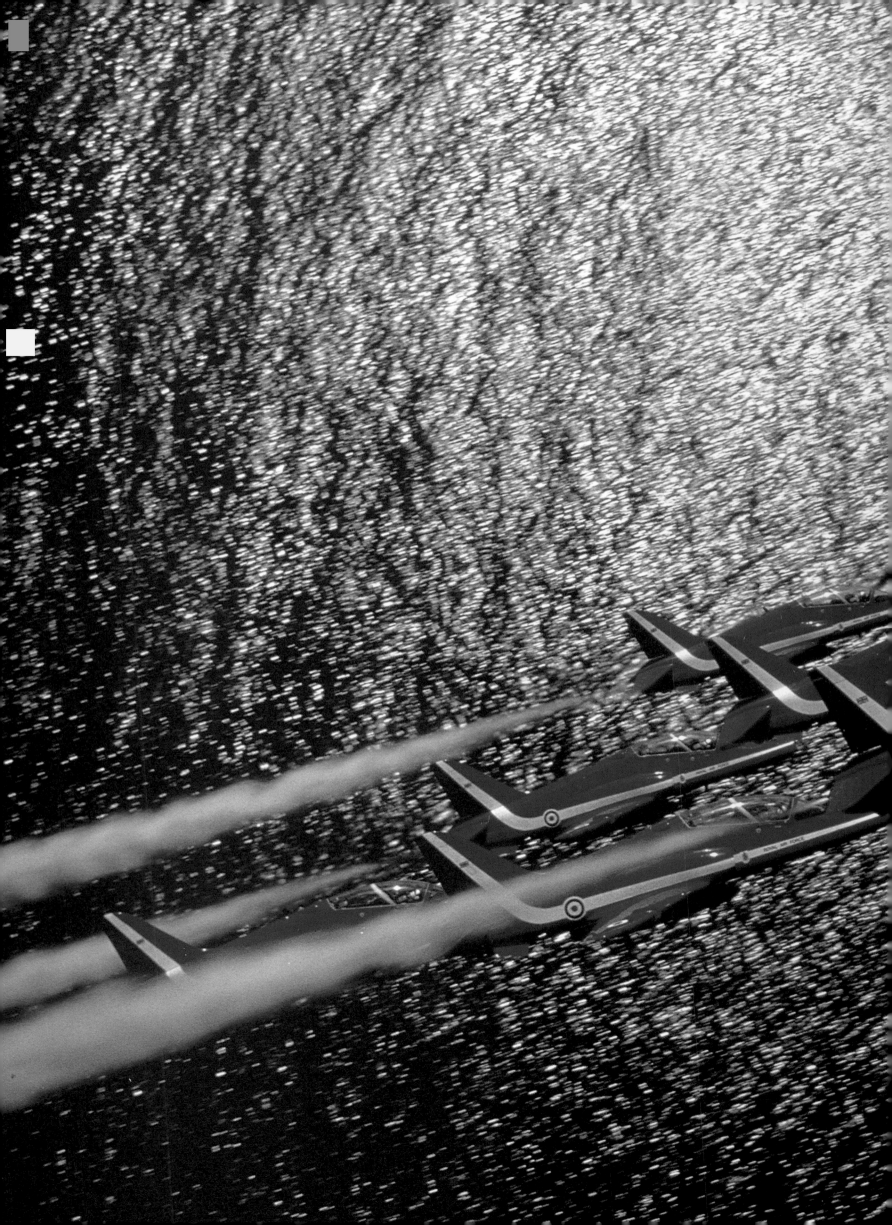

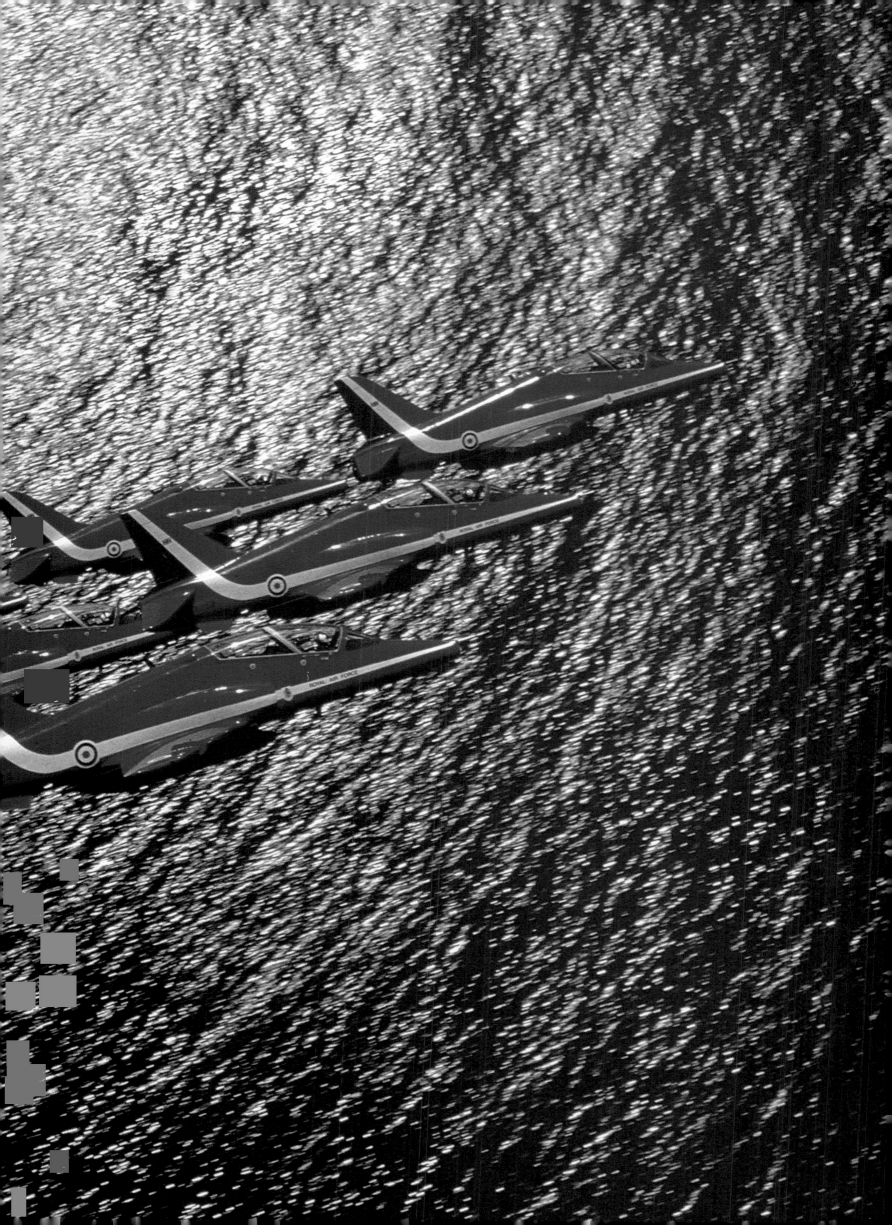

Below *A great deal of practice is required if the Synchro crossing manoeuvres are going to look good from the ground. Every training sortie is video recorded for instant feedback. The pilots can then make minor adjustments, always aiming for the perfect cross.*

Opposite Right *Sparkling "Wineglass".*

P48 *A portrait of the artist hard at work.*

P49 *"Shuttle," renamed in 1990 "Tornado F3" (the RAF's latest fighter aircraft) in recognition of the 50th Anniversary of the Battle of Britain.*

PP50 and 51 *The spectacular end to the "full" display is the "Parasol Break" – known to the pilots as the "Spag"(hetti).*

Opposite *The strength of the team is derived from the skills of each member. Keeping each formation shape cohesive demands intense concentration throughout the whole of the display.*

Below *The objective of the individual is to make the whole look smooth and relaxed.*

PP54 and 55 *"The Rollbacks" during which the pilots pull up in pairs, one from each side of the leader, and roll to the outside of the formation. Eventually everyone is back where they started from.*

PP56 and 57 *Photographed from the rear seat of the Hawk (normally unoccupied during a display) the smoke from other aircraft can be seen in the rear view mirror, trailing out behind us.*

PP58 and 59 *"Feathered Arrow" is something of a mouthful to say over the radio, so we refer to this formation affectionately as "Fred"!*

PP60 and 61 *"Big 9." This is the broadest frontage flown by any aerobatic team, and is the formation in which the Red Arrows arrive to open their displays.*

Left As Synchro describe the outline of a heart, the main section pierces the middle before fanning out in the "Cascade."

Above Red 3 eclipses the sun's reflection from the sea.

PP64 and 65 With their "Tango" formation the Red Arrows became the only Team to roll five aircraft in line abreast and five in line astern at the same time. This dramatic and original photograph, taken directly into the sun, shows that it now takes Nine to Tango!

PP66 and 67 The right hand side of "Big 7", Reds 2, 4 and 8 as seen in the rear-view mirror of the Leader's aircraft. Our own starboard wingtip is also reflected.

Above "The Revolver" is a demanding Synchro manoeuvre. Although it is initially practiced at a comfortable height, the visual cues are not representative for the pilots until they are cleared down to the display height of only 100 feet.

P70 *To ensure that the other eight pilots have sufficient energy (i.e. speed) to maintain control of their aircraft during the slowest stages of the looping manoeuvres, the Leader will only pull up if he has at least 350 knots of airspeed, and even then will only use 4g.*

P71 *The Synchro Pair, however, have the greater flexibility and manoeuvrability of only two aircraft. Synchro 2 (Red 7) can follow Red 6 closely at high "g" levels, and hence fly very tight loops.*

Opposite Rolling "Big Vixen." The Even numbers always fly on the Leader's right, with the odd callsigns flying on his left. In this formation Reds 6 & 7 are astern the Nos 2 & 3.

Below Red 6 emerges from the smoke left by the main section as he completes the crossing manoeuvre known as "The Goose."

PP74 and 75 Most photographs of the Red Arrows are, naturally enough, taken from ground level, and capture the feeling of high speed action. However the opportunity to look down on the display is rare indeed, and from above the salt lake near RAF Akrotiri, Cyprus, one gets instead the impression of graceful precision.

PP76 and 77 The curve of the blue smoke indicates how hard the pilots are "pulling" as they bottom out of the "Tornado Loop." The formation, however, must remain steady.

PP78 and 79 It is a rare pleasure to link up photographically with colleagues flying operational aircraft and it serves as a reminder that all Red Arrows pilots have flown front line aircraft for many years before they join the Team. These are Tornado F3s of No 11(F) Squadron.

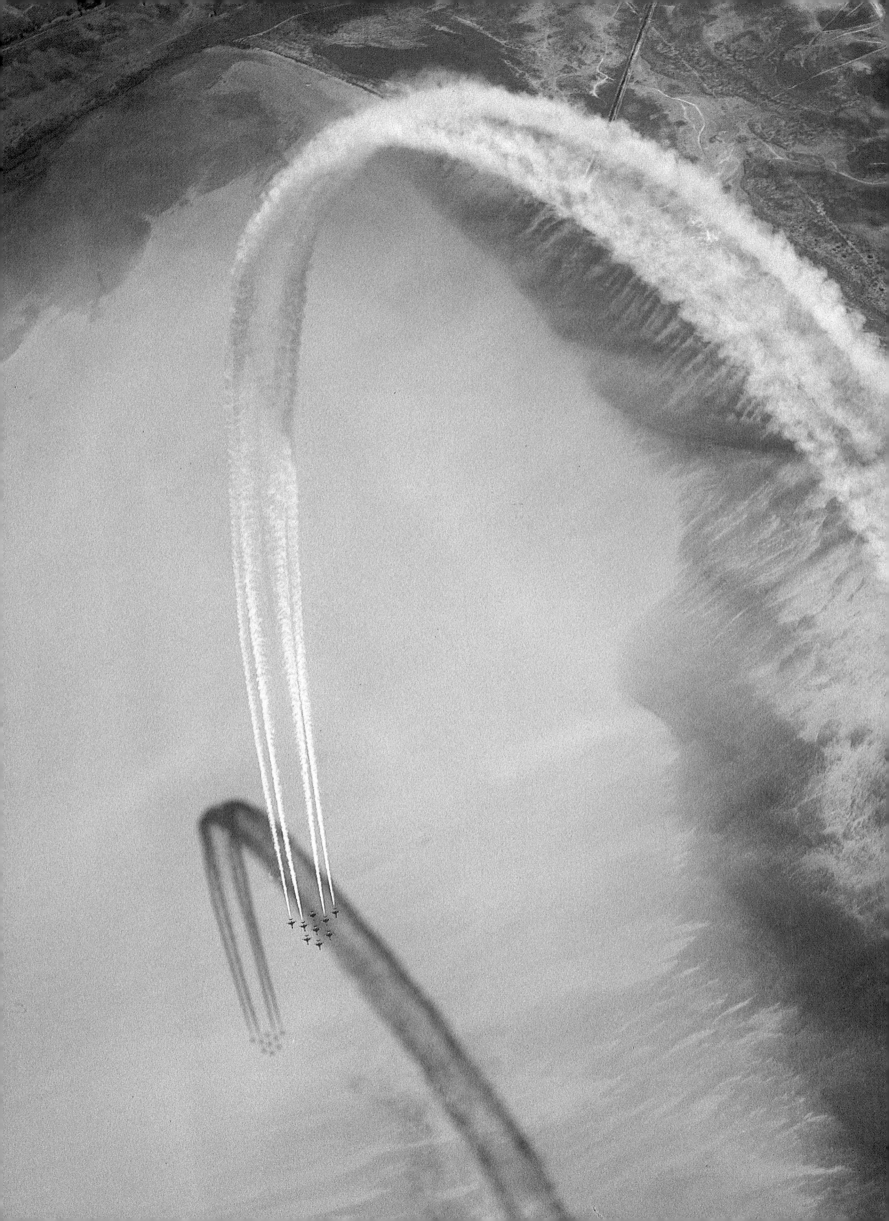

Above, Opposite and PP82 and 83 The Synchro Pair dominate the second half of the display, and offer every photographer the challenge of capturing both their side to side crosses and their head on splits.

PP84 and 85, 86 and 87 Stepped down in "Big 7", looking up the starboard echelon towards the Leader. This is the set up for the "Goose", as we await the Synchro Pair who fly underneath the main formation, with a crossing speed of 600 mph.

Above and Opposite The distance between the aircraft in formation is never more than a few feet, although in line astern successive aircraft fly slightly lower than the one in front, giving separation "in depth." The formation reference for each pilot is precisely defined and an error of more than a few inches in any of the three dimensions will be visible from the ground.

TRAINING AND NEW FORMATIONS

Three new pilots join the team each year and their training begins in earnest in October. During the last month of the previous display season (September) they will have flown with each of the current Team pilots, in the rear seat of their aircraft. Despite the fact that all new team members will have learned to fly the Hawk at some stage during their previous training, the initial weeks are spent re-converting to the aircraft and then becoming acclimatised to looping and rolling in small formations over Scampton airfield. As the pilots' proficiency grows, so the base height is lowered and formation size increased.

Meanwhile, intensive servicing of the aircraft is carried out in rotation so that the pilots' training sorties can progress uninterrupted up to 3 times a day, 5 days a week.

By early February, all of the team's scarlet aircraft are available and the pilots are ready to fly 9-aircraft formations. The Leader can now concentrate on developing a display sequence. Several new ideas will have been tried during the winter, some proving more successful than others! It should be appreciated that there are only so many manoeuvres that can be flown successfully with nine aircraft that keep the display tight, interesting and in an audience's view at all times. For this reason, the display sequence is never completely "new". Each year's show is based on its predecessor, albeit with manoeuvres deleted or inserted and amendments made to the running order. After many years of experimentation, the Red Arrows have tried most of the alternatives!

The work-up training culminates with a detachment to the RAF base in Cyprus where fine weather guarantees continuity of flying and allows the final polish to be put on the display. The full display sequence, flown in good weather, demonstrates well over 20 different formation manoeuvres.

Left The popular "Heart" requires much practice and co-ordination, not only between the Leader and the Synchro Pair, but also between the two Synchro pilots to ensure that the shape is correct.

Above Each training flight, of which there may be up to three per day in the winter, begins with a thorough briefing session. Squadron Leader Adrian Thurley (right) and the Team take advantage of the Cyprus sunshine whilst covering detailed points of the training routine.

Above *The "Display Take Off" is flown in a 3-2-4 sequence prior to forming the Diamond 9. Although not formally part of the display this is often witnessed by air show crowds and as such is practiced to perfection in its own right.*

Below The training day is a long one. Each sortie involves a brief half an hour before take off, a half hour flight and a debrief that can last for as long as an hour. During the winter the three training sessions a day make use of every available daylight hour.

Opposite The first "nine ship" of the year is not normally flown until early February, when all the aircraft have returned from winter servicing, and the new pilots are ready to be integrated into a large formation.

PP96 and 97 "Tango" features five aircraft in line abreast and five in line astern, and as such is one of the hardest shapes to fly. The Red Arrows are the only Team in the world to roll five aircraft in line astern, as Red 9, here barely visible at the back, keeps reminding the rest of us!

PP98 and 99 The gatefold at the beginning of this book shows the Twizzle viewed from abeam the Leader. When viewed from above, tiny differences in technique used by different pilots show as errors that must be ironed out during training.

PP100 and 101 The full display opens with a pull up from Big 9 (see pages 60/61) into a loop during which the Diamond is formed. This first dynamic formation change sets the tone for the show and must be carried out swiftly and precisely in full view of the audience. Captured here is the moment that Reds 6 and 7 (third from the right and left) begin to move to take up positions astern the Leader.

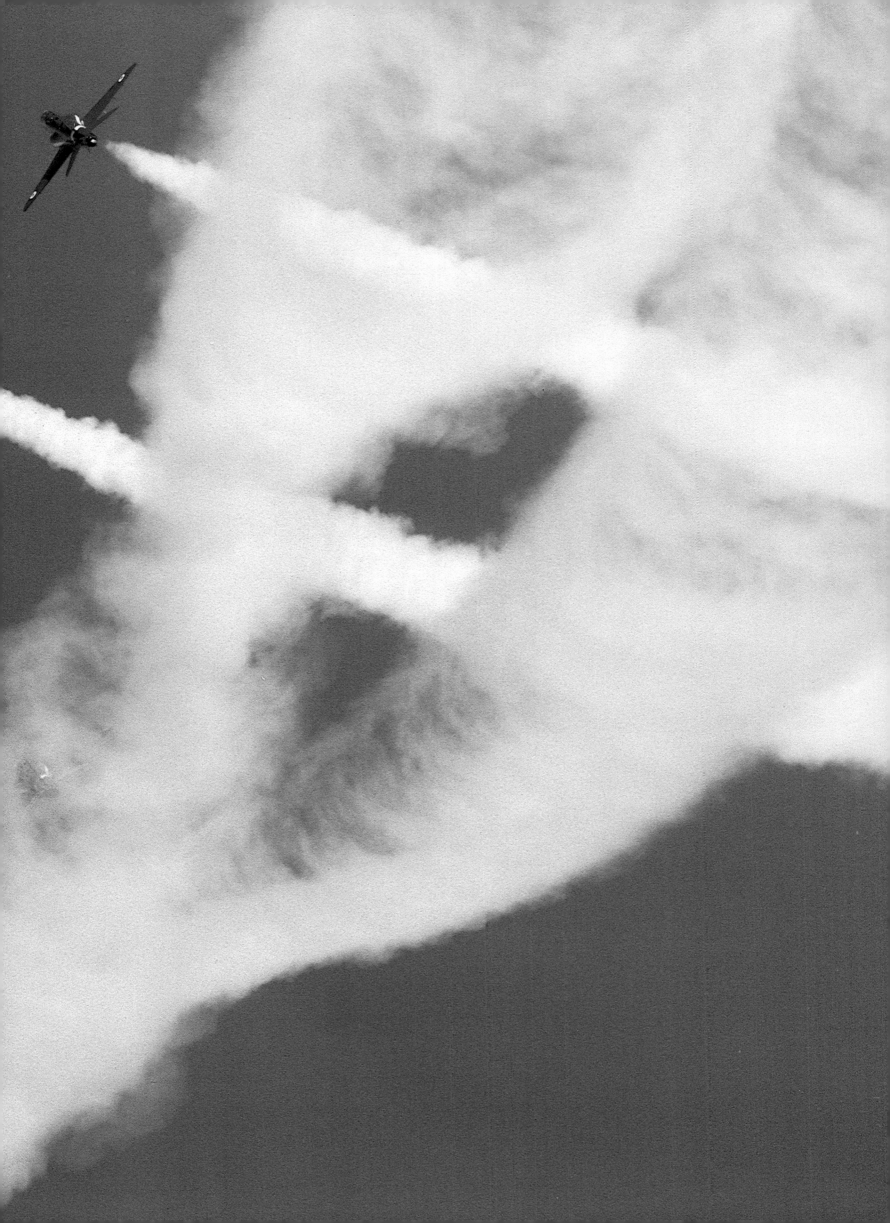

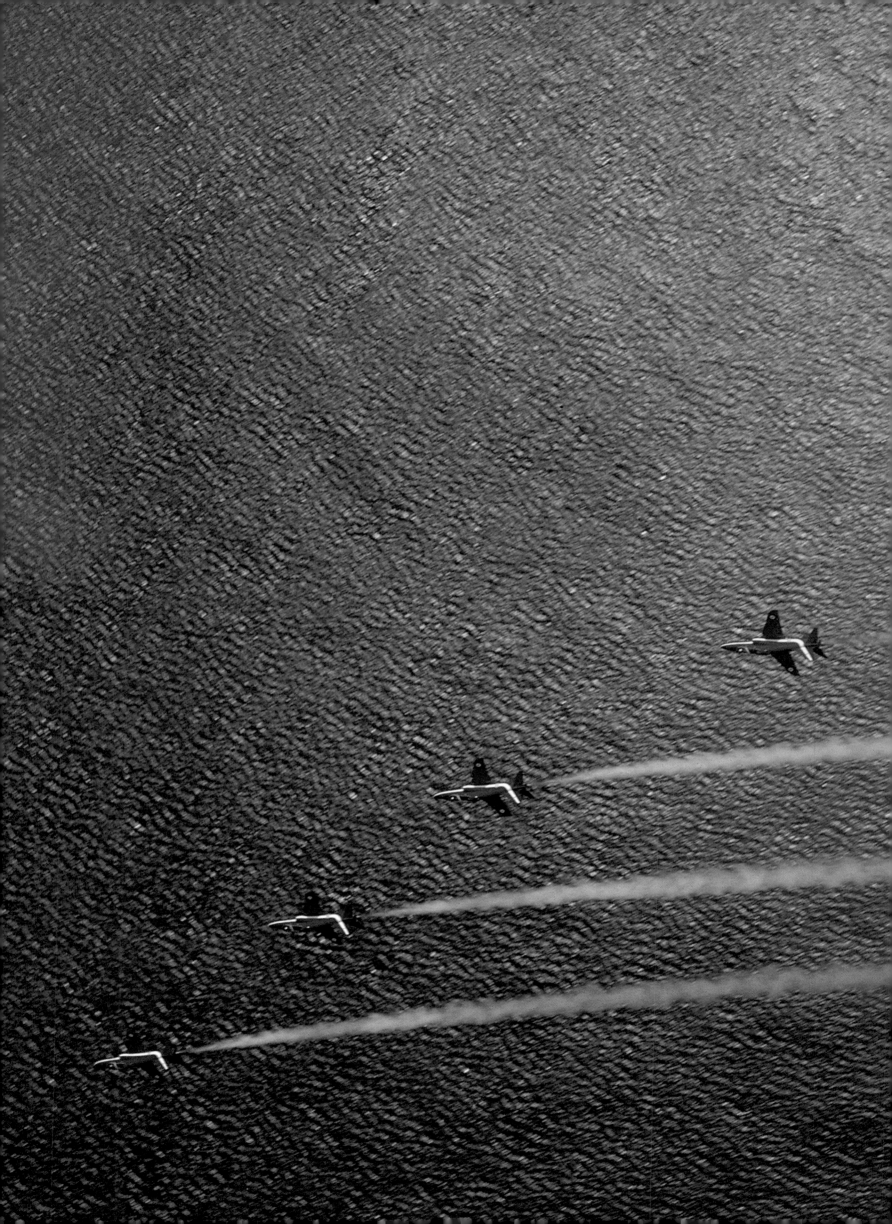

Above Each leader of the Synchro Pair was last season's Synchro 2. During the display, these 2 pilots will fly inverted at just 100 feet, and so must be comfortable with viewing an upside down world. Here the new Red 7 practices inverted formation flying!

Left The transformation from "Big 9" to "Diamond" at the beginning of the show (pages 100/101) is completed when Reds 8 and 9 move astern Reds 2 and 3, leaving Reds 4 and 5 on the right and left tips of this shape.

PP104 and 105 The T shape (pages 96/97) seen in recent years is a development from "Delta" and "Wineglass", both of which involve five aircraft flying in line abreast. Changing just two of the aircraft positions (Reds 8 and 9) effectively alters the whole formation shape. The designs are always symmetrical, and so the slightest error is very obvious.

PP106 and 107 A different view of "Wineglass". The "stem" are now perfectly matched but the front row is still not quite in line. The pilots are very aware of any minor errors in the air and will strive to correct them as quickly as they occur, such that most onlookers would not have noticed any imbalance. The still photograph however, captures forever a momentary error of judgement!

PP108 and 109 "Viggen", which was renamed for the 1990 season as "Flanker", the NATO codename for the Soviet Su-27 aircraft. In that year the Team made its first visit to the USSR.

Above The "caterpillar," which involves seven aircraft in a sequential pull up into a tail-chase loop, requires a clear sky and is therefore only ever seen during the good weather shows. Despite the frustrations imposed by our European weather, the swirl of white smoke occasionally contrasts with the colours of a clear summers day.

Opposite The "Apollo" loop, with Red 3 closest to the camera and Reds 5 and 9 trailing red smoke. Originally honouring the NASA space capsule, itself named after the Greek sun god, this formation's poetic title has another appropriate definition; serene, thoughtful and self-disciplined.

RECTIFICATION GROUND CREW

Throughout the display season the Squadron's rectification ground crew, who do not normally travel with the Team, provide the diagnostic skill and practical expertise to maintain the aircraft between detachments. The 40 technicians who make up the "Second Line" of engineers offer a variety of trades and specialist knowledge, and are commanded by a Flight Lieutenant. There are often only a few days between detachments during which all the aircraft must be restored to pristine condition and prepared for the next deployment. Should an aircraft develop a serious problem while detached, a team of technicians from the rectification crew is quickly dispatched to recover it.

The rectification ground crew really show their expertise during the winter. In the space of the five months from October to February, each Hawk aircraft is given an extensive overhaul, lasting some four weeks. With the aircraft dismantled the various systems are inspected and tested in an effort to minimise routine maintenance and the likelihood of any technical problems arising during the season. The timely completion of "Winter Servicing" is essential to ensure that all the aircraft are ready for the forthcoming season, and that pilot training is therefore not disrupted.

TRAVELLING GROUND CREW

The travelling ground crew, usually referred to as the "First Line," are a close knit team of 27 dedicated and skilled tradesmen. Commanded by a Flight Lieutenant Engineering Officer (the only non-pilot Team member to wear the coveted Red Flying Suit), they are each responsible for different specific engineering tasks. Their open air working conditions are often difficult with tasks having to be carried out quickly in order to prepare the aircraft for the next flight, allowing the performance of up to three displays in a day.

Nine of the tradesmen and the Engineering Officer are in the "Circus," which means that they each fly as a passenger in the Hawk on transit flights. Each Circus member works with the same pilot throughout the season and is responsible for his aircraft's flight servicing as well as for the preparation of that pilot's flying kit.

Equally as important as the Circus are the remainder of the First Line Engineering Team who travel in the support Hercules or by road transport. They provide the specialist support needed to rectify any minor faults that occur en route or during the display, and it is at these times that they really come into their own.

During the winter months First Line is scaled down to half strength, operating what is known as a "Winter Line." The remainder of the First Line move across to Second Line to assist with the winter servicing of the team's Hawk aircraft.

By the end of January, First Line is back to full strength and all tasks for the coming display season have been allocated. This is a very intensive build up period when the new ground support crews work up to speed for the following display season.

Above *Pre dawn on a cold winter's day in Lincolnshire and the engineers are at work two hours before the aircrew, collectively preparing the aircraft for their first flight.*

Opposite *During the summer display season ten fortunate engineers become "The Circus," and are appointed one to each of the aircraft. Wearing blue flying suits, they transit to the display site or forward operating airfield in the back seats of the aircraft.*

PP116 and 117 Each travelling engineer has a specific trade skill (e.g. propulsion, airframe, electrics etc) and when away from base becomes the "on the road expert" in his field, should problems be encountered.

P118 The groundcrew are a vital element in the Team and often go unnoticed by the crowds. However they lavish great care and attention on "their" aircraft, which they then allow the pilots to borrow! Without them the show could not go on.

P119 The workhorse of the Team, on overseas trips or during very busy schedules at home, is the C-130 Hercules. Transporting engineers, spares, dye (for the coloured smoke) luggage, publicity material and support vehicles, the "Herc" becomes home for several days at a time. Here the captain displays a souvenir on our return from a fascinating tour of the Soviet Union. You do not often see the Hammer and Sickle on an RAF aircraft!

PP120 and 121 The day may have included two or three displays already, but we still plan to move on to the next show site if at all possible. At least then we can begin each day in the right place.

PP122 and 123 "The Rollbacks," captured just as two aircraft are pulling up and away from the Leader. They then roll to the outsides of "Big 7," eventually to return to their original positions.

Above Whatever the weather or time of day, the Team always puts maximum effort into each display and therefore into pleasing its millions of admirers.

Opposite Farewell from the Red Arrows, as they divide the sky into nine equal segments in the show stopping "Parasol Break."

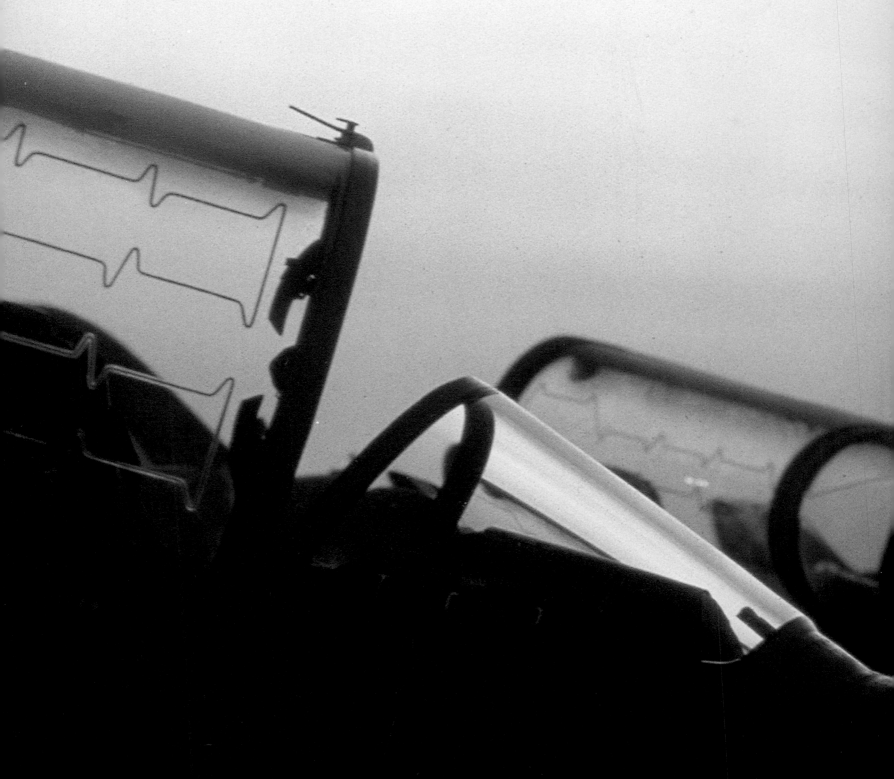